Wolfgang Reuter
The Lipizzaners and the
Spanish Riding School

The Lipizzaners and the Spanish Riding School

Wolfgang Reuter

Pinguin-Verlag, Innsbruck

The publishers are particularly indebted to the photographic archives
of the Ministry of Agriculture and Forestry for supplying the colour photographs.
© 1983 by Pinguin-Verlag
A-6021 Innsbruck
Printed by M. Theiss, A-9400 Wolfsberg
Lithography: Ifolith, Innsbruck
Printed in Austria
ISBN 3-7016-2145-6

Contents

The history of the Lipizzaner breed

The Lipizzaner takes its name from the original Lipizza stud which is situated on Yugoslavian territory and which still exists today.

The Karst region around Trieste already enjoyed an outstanding reputation for horse breeding in the days of classical antiquity. This must have been Archduke Charles of Hapsburg's main reason for founding a stud there in 1580, near the village of Lipizza, to breed Spanish horses.

The Spanish horse was originally produced during the Moorish rule by crossing Berber and Arab stallions with mares of the indigenous Iberian breed. It had all the qualities demanded of an ideal mount at that time and was very popular among riders on account of its elegant movements, its firm build and its above-average aptitude for haute école training.

Thus it was that the ruling houses of Europe established studs for the breeding of Spanish horses. These included Frederiksborg, the Danish stud, the Lippe-Bückeburg stud in Germany and Kladrub an der Elbe stud in the Hapsburg crown-lands. The latter stud concentrated on rearing carriage-horses of a large build, however.

Kladrub still exists in Czechoslovakia and Kladrubers are still bred there, carriage-horses or coach-horses with a large frame, once required by royalty for festive and funeral processions. Kladrub was important for the Lipizzaner breed in that it provided one of the principal sires, the renowned Maestoso whose blood still flows today in the veins of the Maestoso line.

But it was without doubt Lipizza which acquired the greatest significance as a breeding site for Spanish horses used as mounts.

In the year of its foundation Baron Khevenhiller purchased 24 mares and nine stallions, the basis of the stud. With this first horse importation all the requirements for an auspicious beginning had been created. Construction work was set about with a will and by 1585 all the buildings and equipment for the stud farm had been installed. Six large cisterns had been made to catch rainwater, an effective way of dealing with the tiresome water shortage. The stables and accommodation had been built, a wall enclosing them, and part of the stony ground had been made into fertile soil. By 1595 it was possible to send thirty foals to the ducal stud at Graz.

In the course of the years the founder's successors enlarged the stud, purchasing new Spanish horses to ensure that the breed acquired fresh blood. The stud's first brilliant era came during the reign of Emperor Leopold I, a baroque ruler with a love of splendour who required numerous horses as mounts and as carriage-horses for his court. He took upon himself the task of expanding the Karst stud. His breeding rules issued in 1658 showed an expert knowledge of the subject and can still be regarded as exemplary today. They proved so beneficial for Lipizza that there was soon a surplus of horses.

The reigns of Emperor Leopold I and Charles VI saw the purchase of those famous sires, Cordova (1701), Generale (1710), Amico (1712), Danese (1718), Superbo (1722) and Montedoro (1739). Pluto, the original Dane (1772), and Conversano, the original Neapolitan

(1774), came to Lipizza as sires during Maria Theresia's reign. 150 brood mares were kept there at that time. All of the stallions purchased were of pure Spanish descent, despite the fact that they were imported from Denmark, Germany and Italy.

The Lipizzaners' flight

The royal stud developed undisturbed until 1785. Then a period of misfortune began.

First came a petition from Herr von Breinl, seriously proposing that the stud at Lipizza be dissolved and a similar establishment be installed in Galicia. Emperor Joseph II rejected this application.

Later, in March 1792, the entire stud had to be evacuated to Stuhlweißenburg, Hungary, in the face of the French advance. The 300 horses survived the 14-day march without loss. The hardiness of the Karst horses had passed the test. In October of the same year the horses returned home. But the French had destroyed all the stud buildings and equipment as well as the complete stud archives, an irreplaceable loss to posterity.

Rebuilding commenced at once, but on 4th January 1802 an earthquake again reduced the buildings to ruins. Hardly had the stables and farm buildings been put up again when, in 1805, the French threatened the stud for a second time, necessitating the removal of the horses to Diakovar in Slavonia and thence to Karjad. In 1807 the horses returned, remaining at home for two years.

Following the Treaty of Vienna in 1809, under which Trieste and Carinthia were ceded to the French, the Lipizzaners had to leave their meadows and stables once more, undertaking the long march to Pecska in Hungary between 13th May and 17th June. For six years the refugees were to remain there in the Theiss plain. The climatic conditions were not favourable for these Karst horses and it seemed that the breed would lose its identity and die out.

Then, in 1815, salvation came with the order for the return march and soon the valuable horses were reinstalled in their own, albeit dilapidated, home stables. The horses visibly recovered. By systematic pairing and selection, the breed soon regained its earlier standard. Maestoso from Kladrub, mentioned above, proved particularly useful as the principal sire.

The final century as a royal stud

Until the First World War Lipizza was spared further setbacks.

The stud was still the subject of various intrigues, the last of these in the reign of Emperor Franz Joseph I, but the Hapsburgs had always been great horse lovers and this monarch was no exception. He ensured that the stud could continue and its final heyday came during his reign.

The emperor loved the Karst horses and his carriages were drawn exclusively by Lipizzaners. These "Lipizzanerjucker", as they are known to the experts, were the result of cross-breeding with the Arab stallions Tadmor, Gazlan, Benazet, Samson, Hadudi, Saydan and Siglavy. The main reason for this manner of breeding was the conviction that the Lipizzaners urgently needed fresh blood. Since original Spanish horses were no longer available in the 19th century, Arabs were chosen. Siglavy, purchased in 1816, was the only one to found a separate line, however. This period at the stud was altogether marked by a great readiness to experiment. The English thoroughbred had just started its triumphal progress across Europe and was to prove its worth in Lipizza, too. Cross-breeding experiments did not show the desired results and the progeny were allowed to die out.

In around 1870 the stud farm numbered 5 stallions and 98 mares.

The stallions employed were:
1. at any given time one pure Lipizzaner out of the Conversano, Pluto, Favory, Maestoso and Neapolitano strains in turn
2. Gazlan, a thoroughbred Arab purchased in Syria
3. Samson, a thoroughbred Arab purchased in the Gaza region
4. Benazet, a thoroughbred Arab bred in Galicia
5. Northern Light, an English cross-breed

The mares were:
26 Lipizzaner mares of pure Karst stock
26 Arab mares
46 cross-breed mares

Three strains of horse were bred from the stallions and mares listed above—Arabs, Lipizzaners and a cross-breed of the two. Some of the Arabs were desert horses, some had been reared in Europe. The cross-breeds were descendants of Arab stallions and either pure Lipizzaner or cross-bred mares. The mating period lasted from December to the end of May. Fertility was very high and the number of barren mares did not generally exceed ten per cent. The foals were given hay and oats with their dam's milk and were weaned at five months. Between the end of May and the beginning of November the horses were put out to graze, but were given additional hay. In early March of their fourth year the horses went to Vienna to the Spanish Riding School and to the Imperial Stables for whose exclusive use they were intended. The best brood mares were picked out beforehand, however, and used for breeding on the stud farm.

The two World Wars

With Italy's entry into the War in 1915 the Lipizza royal stud was now in the immediate area of the fighting. An imperial decree ordered that the horses be "temporarily moved". The brood mares, sires, four-year-old mares and service horses were taken to Laxenburg outside Vienna, whilst the yearlings, colts and fillies alike, went to Kladrub in Bohemia.

The end of the First World War signified the fall of the Danube Monarchy and the dissolution of the court treasury. The last Hapsburg emperor—and this dynasty had always been concerned that the Lipizzaners be saved—went into exile.

The young Republic had a great struggle to ensure the continued existence of the Spanish Riding School and the Lipizzaner stock, for the Treaty of Versailles had awarded Lipizza to Italy and that country was now demanding the return of the entire breeding stock. 107

horses were handed over to Italy. The remaining ninety-seven were taken to Piber near Graz where Lipizzaner breeding was continued at the National Stud Farm as from 1920.

At the outbreak of the Second World War in 1939 the following Lipizzaner studs existed in addition to Piber and Lipizza:

1. Babolna in Hungary with 40 mares and 4 stallions
2. Topolcianky in Czechoslovakia with 2 sires and 30 mares
3. Fogoras in Rumania with 50 mares and 5 stallions
4. Stancic, Kruschedol and Demir Kapja in Yugoslavia with 70 brood mares and 6 stallions

During the Second World War 40 mares, 3 sires and the yearlings were transferred from Piber to Hostau in the Bohemian Forest. The bloodstock from Lipizza and the Yugoslavian Lipizzaner studs were also moved there to protect them from the partisans and foreign troops. Piber was to be used as a breeding site for mountain horses.

With its extensive estates and its modern buildings, Hostau provided the ideal conditions for horse breeding, even if it lacked Piber's rough mountain pastures. It is thus difficult to assess the effects of soil and climate on the quality of the horses. One fact is undisputed, however: Hostau produced several talented dressage horses for the Spanish Riding School and many fine mares for Piber.

At the end of the War the situation in Hostau became increasingly difficult with the approach of the Red Army. The competent authorities refused permission for the valuable breeding stock to be evacuated and the irreplaceable Lipizzaners were threatened with extinction, like the main part of Trakehnen stud at the beginning of 1945.

This desperate situation was saved at the last minute by the Americans who were positioned to the west of Hostau, very near the former German border with Czechoslovakia. They were aware of the existence of the stud and its valuable bloodstock and they were prepared to help.

Negotiations between the competent German veterinary officers and officers from the American advance units were marked by a great love of horses on both sides and paved the way for the handing over of Hostau to the Americans.

General Patton, the commanding officer of the American troops, gave permission for the advance into, as yet, unoccupied territory, territory really belonging to the Soviet sphere of interest. On 28th April, 1945 American units under Colonel Reed occupied Hostau. Arrangements were made for the evacuation of the Lipizzaners. This took place in the early hours of 12th May and was completed late in the night of that day in the safety of Bavaria. Since there were insufficient vehicles available, several small groups were formed, each of these being accompanied by an American military vehicle at the head and at the rear. The outriders were German stud employees, American soldiers and Cossacks who had halted at Hostau on their flight to the West. The only horses to be transported in lorries were brood mares with very young foals. All the Lipizzaners were taken safely and more or less without incident from Hostau to Schwarzenburg, Bavaria. There, the Lipizzaners from Piber were quickly identified by Colonel Podhajsky, director of the Spanish Riding School. At his request they were taken to St. Martin in Upper Austria.

After the evacuation of the Spanish Riding School from Vienna St. Martin had served as a refuge from the bombing and from the advancing Russians. It was here that that memorable performance of the Spanish Riding School took place before General Patton, the occasion for Colonel Podhajsky to request American Army protection for the Riding School and the Lipizzaners. Patton, the horse lover, agreed and arranged for the director of the Spanish Riding School to be flown by military aircraft to a meeting with Colonel Reed in Zinkovy, Czechoslovakia. Reed had been responsible for moving the Lipizzaners from Hostau to Bavaria.

At this meeting Reed promised his support for the return of the former Piber bloodstock to Austria.

Later this somewhat precipitate transport to St. Martin was repeatedly criticized because several horses were seriously injured and two mares had to be shot. All those involved acted with the best of intentions, however, it being of paramount importance that the Lipizzaners should be taken back to their home in Austria.

Thanks are due to General Patton for his magnificent assistance which saved the Lipizzaner stud and the Spanish Riding School. Austria and the world of equestrianism are grateful to General Patton for his fairness.

No sooner had the guns of the Second World War been silenced than the Lippizaners were able to move back to Piber, their native stud. The Spanish Riding School remained in St. Martin for some time, however, and then spent several years in Wels. After the signing of the Austrian State Treaty it returned to Vienna.

The Lipizzaner stud at Piber

At the national stud farm in Piber Lipizzaners are reared in the traditional manner of the Austrian show and parade horse of yore. This type of horse once gave Hapsburg court ceremonial its special stamp and was used for tournaments and festive processions, too.

Piber has proved to be an excellent substitute for Lipizza. Today three sires and 43 brood mares are used for breeding.

The six old-established lines of descent still exist. They go back to the stallions Pluto, Conversano, Neapolitano, Favory, Maestoso and Siglavy, all of which passed down very characteristic features. It is thus easy to distinguish between the various lines of descent by outward appearance. The Plutos, their ancestors from Spain and Denmark, are sturdy horses with a rectangular build, ram-like heads and a high set neck. The Conversanos have Arab blood, strong ram-like heads, a short back, broad hocks and dignified movements. The Maestosos are powerful horses with a long back, extremely muscular cruppers and heavy heads. Despite their strain of Arab blood the Neapolitanos were able to retain their original features. Tall and more rangy in appearance, they have graceful

Brood mares with foals at Piber (top) and young stallions on the Stubalm

movements and a high action. The Arab influence is more noticeable in the Favorys, their lighter build being a sign of this. The soft curve of their nose still calls to mind their Kladrub progenitor, however, a true Spanish horse. The Siglavys typify the Arab Lipizzaner with aristocratic heads, a slender neck, high withers and a relatively short back.

All the descendants of the various lines have in common an attractive, albeit baroque, appearance, graceful movements, a lively temperament, a wonderful nature and an outstanding aptitude for the lessons of the haute école. Their height varies from 15 to 16½ hands (61 to 66 in.). Their hard, well-formed hooves, steely tendons and sturdy bones provide them with a capacity for work which is indispensable in dressage training and which is the result of selective breeding for several centuries. The use of Arab stallions to provide fresh blood resulted in the predominantly white colour which they have today. In previous centuries there were many blacks, browns, duns, piebalds and skewbalds among the Lipizzaners, however. Nowadays brown Lipizzaners are relatively rare, but it has become a tradition to work with at least one brown stallion in the Spanish Riding School.

Like all white horses, the foals are born brown, dark brown or mouse grey, acquiring their white coat gradually between their 7th and 10th years. The last dark hair to go is that in their manes and tails. Thus it is possible to make a rough estimate of a horse's age from its colouring.

The horses have L branded on the lower left jaw and P with the crown on the left hind quarters. Brands indicating their paternal and maternal descent are applied to the saddle area. The first half of the stallions' double name is the name of their sire and the second half that of their dam. The old Lipizza breeding regulations are still followed in Piber. The only stallions used for breeding are those which have "passed their exams" in the Spanish Riding School. In this respect the Lipizzaner differs considerably from horses of other breeds. The proficiency of the stallions is put to the test over several years and provides precise information as to the quality of the future sire. The brood mares, colts and fillies are kept in large unpartitioned stables so that, even at the time of year when grazing is not possible, they have great freedom of movement. During the summer months the mares and foals are put out to graze twice a day. During the midday heat they remain in the stables, however. There they are watered and given additional oats and hay.

For visitors to the stud farm it is an unforgettable sight when the brood mares return to the stables in the evening. Only supervised by a few stud employees, each mare with her foal at once finds her own place in the correct stable.

In the first three and a half years of their life the colts and fillies are moved up to the stud's mountain pastures at the end of May. They remain there, at an altitude of 1,600 m, until the end of September.

The period spent on these steep and stony mountain pastures ensures tough conditions similar to those of yore in Lipizza, although the climate up at these altitudes is certainly more raw than it was on those karst meadows.

The four-year-old mares are broken in and, if they are found suitable for breeding purposes, they join the famous string of brood mares. The young stallions are moved to the Spanish Riding School in Vienna in their fourth year. There they receive the same training as was customary during the Hapsburg era.

Mutterstuten in Lipizza im Jahre 1727, Gemälde von J. G. Hamilton, Wien, Spanische Reitschule
Brood mares in Lipizza in 1727, painting by J. G. Hamilton, Spanish Riding School, Vienna

Stute „Perla" mit ihrem 4 Tage alten Fohlen im Staatsgestüt Piber
Perla, the mare, with her 4-day-old foal at the National Stud, Piber

Stutenherde in Lipizza, Gemälde von Julius von Blaas, 1898, Wien, Spanische Reitschule
Mares at Lipizza, Painting by Julius von Blaas, 1898, Spanish Riding School, Vienna

Equestrianism
from antiquity to the
present day

The art of riding was already highly regarded in classical antiquity and had reached a high standard of development even then. The oldest surviving equestrian principles were laid down by Xenophon. His two works, "The Guide to Riding" and "The Art of Horsemanship" were written in around 400 B.C. and remained the only written works on horsemanship until the 16th century. Xenophon's teachings were intended for the training of war horses. They were the result of careful observation and much practical experience.

Of the war horse Xenophon demanded greater co-operation and obedience than many a horse at dressage trials today is capable of showing.

His insistence on a command of the haunches, thus ensuring the horse's tractability during the thick of battle, constitutes the basic element of classic equestrianism. Xenophon's riding principles are still valid today. That does not mean that horsemanship has stood still, but it does underline that great Greek's brilliant conception and accurate judgement regarding the training of horses.

Unfortunately Xenophon's teachings were to sink gradually into oblivion in the subsequent course of history. During the confusion accompanying the period of tribal migration equestrian art was driven ever further into the background in ancient Rome. Chariot racing had become the main focus of interest. In the end the Romans had to learn how to manage war horses again from the Teutons, although little emphasis was placed on Xenophon's principles there.

During the Middle Ages the art of dressage was but little in demand. The heavily burdened tournament horses were required to charge forward in a straight line and to help unseat the opponent by the greatest possible force of impact.

We first find a rebirth of interest in horsemanship with the invention of firearms. Cavalry warfare required agile horses, trained in the arts of the haute école. Many of the exercises demonstrated today in the Spanish Riding School in Vienna date back to that period:

The obedient stallion rescued its rider from a desperate situation in battle by means of a capriole, at the same time repulsing the pursuer with a blow of the hooves. In the levade he uses his own body to protect his master from the enemy fire. An elegant pirouette enabled the pursuer to overtake his fleeing enemy and to challenge him to do battle. Thus the horses took an active part in the fighting and their skill and unwavering obedience decided the victory or defeat of their riders.

The first new impetus for haute école came from Italy when Frederico Grisone, a Neapolitan nobleman, published a new work on horsemanship in 1550. In England it was the Duke of Newcastle who concerned himself with dressage, although the responsibility for having ruined English riders' taste for haute école must be laid at his door. The cause of this was that the Duke preached a foreshortening of all the movements. Horse-racing was becoming very fashionable in England at that time and the duke's ideas fell on stony ground. In Germany a book on horsemanship written by Georg Engelhardt von Löhneysen appeared in

1588. France's contribution to the art of riding came from Pluvinel, Gaspart de Saunier and F. R. de la Guérinière. The latter thoroughly reformed riding, introducing the dressage riding position in place of the "open" position so that the rider's thighs could now be used for guidance. Guérinière rode all his horses with soft bits. For him relaxation and continuity were of prime importance and prerequisite for the horse's obedience.

Schecke (Cerbero) in der Kapriole, Gemälde nach Art des G. Hamilton, Wien, Spanische Reitschule
A piebald horse (Cerbero) in a capriole, painting in the manner of G. Hamilton, Spanish Riding School,
Vienna

Brauner in der Piaffe, Gemälde nach Art des G. Hamilton, Wien, Spanische Reitschule
A bay executing a piaffe, painting in the manner of G. Hamilton, Spanish Riding School, Vienna

A noble setting
for
a noble horse

The Vienna Court Riding School, or Hofreitschule, can look back on a long history: In 1565 mention is made of a "Roßtumplplatz", an exercise ground for horses. Apparently they were originally trained in the open air, but in 1572 the existence of a "Spanish Riding Hall" was first recorded. The manège was now housed in a wooden building so that the horses could be ridden and trained there during the winter months. Since only horses of Spanish descent were used for the haute école, the term "Spanish Riding School" came to be used. Today, too, the only horses trained in the Riding School are Lipizzaners, descendants of that famous Spanish breed.

An imperial command of 1681 ordered the construction of a permanent riding school. It was to be installed on the ground floor of the Court Library and riding was to commence there in the winter of 1685. The Turkish Wars repeatedly delayed this project, however, and finally it was given up. Eventually the lovely baroque building for the Winter Riding School was built between 1729 and 1735 to Joseph Emanuel Fischer von Erlach's design. It stood on that spot indicated as the "Pleasure Garden of His Majesty the Roman King" on an old plan of Vienna dating back to 1547.

The Riding School hall is revealed to visitors as a magnificent room, flooded with light. It has two galleries and a wonderful, richly ornamented stucco ceiling.

Opposite the entrance is the portrait of Empéror Charles VI mounted on a Lipizzaner stallion. This provides the only patch of colour on the walls of the hall. The manège of the Vienna Hofreitschule was always regarded as one of the loveliest throughout Europe. It became the festive setting for many grand celebrations, riding tournaments and splendid carriage parades. The last carousel staged here during the monarchy was in 1894 under the patronage of Emperor Francis Jospeh I. This was a special occasion in that riders who were commoners were allowed to take part for the first time. Part of the festive programme included a school quadrille with four horses ridden by the head rider and riders from the Spanish Riding School. From then on the Winter Riding School was used exclusively for the cultivation of classical equestrianism and the training of the Lipizzaner stallions.

Less well known is the so-called Summer Riding School which is situated between the Schatzkammer (treasury), the Redoutensaal, the south-west front of the Winter Riding School and the State Chancery wing of the Hofburg. In a setting of tall buildings and shady trees, this idyllic riding ground is an oasis of peace in the midst of the big city. In the spring and summer the horses are usually ridden here until 10 a.m., then it is time for morning work with the horses in the covered manège and before an audience.

Carousel on 21st April, 1894. "The Entry of Charles VI", from a drawing by M. Ledeli

The Royal and Imperial Riding School in 1880, surveyed and drawn by G. Niemann

The Spanish
Riding School

Nobody can forget the occasion of his first visit to the Spanish Riding School. Iron discipline and time-honoured tradition are the rule here, in the world's oldest riding school. Fischer von Erlach's magnificent building provides a setting unequalled anywhere else. Before the eyes of the spectator is revealed a world far removed from the bustle of everyday life and radiating that tranquillity which is essential for work with horses. No word is spoken. Only the dull thud of hooves and the creak of leather mingles with the heavy breathing of the stallions. Everyone goes about his duty unobtrusively. In the traditional brown dress coat, white buckskin breeches, black top-boots and bicorn hat, the riders work their horses without any ostentation. All ride in the classic Viennese style which has produced so many outstanding riders. The leading actors, the white stallions, dominate the scene. Poised in the air, they seem quite detached from the ground and bear witness to the high standard of haute ecole in the Spanish Riding School.

At present there are 75 stallions in the stables of the Spanish Riding School and these include three brown. The head riding master supervises the work with the horses. He is assisted by three riding masters, five riders, five rider candidates and four trainees.

The training plan at the Spanish Riding School has always been based on F. R. de la Guérinière's principles. For centuries responsibility for the training of the horses has lain in the hands of the riding masters. It is thanks to them that classic equestrianism has been kept alive right up to the present day. In the course of their apprenticeship they acquired a wealth of experience to pass on to the next generation of riders.

Even today great emphasis is placed on the training of new riding masters.

The faultless seat which we admire in the riders of the Spanish Riding School is the result of systematic practice on the lunging rein. Even the experts use this frequently to correct any faults which may have arisen in their manner of sitting. The correct seat is imperative for guidance of the horse and for the general appearance. By riding the older, more experienced horses, the young rider becomes familiar with the lessons of the haute école and acquires a feeling for using the right aids. The horse becomes the rider's teacher and this learning from the horse is invaluable. The intelligent stallion notices every mistake and the beginner's smallest weakness, of course. Great self-discipline is thus required on the part of the pupil so that he can keep himself under control when an exercise goes wrong. On no account must he blame the horse for the fault, but must strive to give guidance as precise as that which the stallion once learnt from the experienced riding master. For it is the expert instructors at the School who instil their knowledge into the young horses, patiently and diligently transforming them into well schooled stallions.

This tradition of training for rider and horse is of great practical value for the Spanish Riding School. The novice rider learns from the horse, and the horse from the trainer. This interplay has enabled classical equestrianism to be cultivated down through the centuries in Vienna.

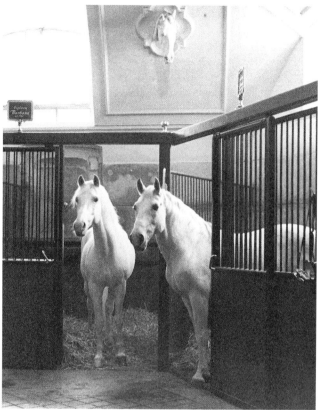

Brigadier Kurt Albrecht with his favourites in the stables

The aim of the work at the Spanish Riding School has always been the cultivation of classical equestrianism at its greatest level of perfection.

It was, of course, with first-class riding instruction for their sons in mind that the Hapsburgs founded the Riding School. Since only the very best instructors with outstanding ability were employed, classical equestrianism survived for centuries. The training of the Lipizzaner stallions provided an opportunity for the nobility to perfect their riding abilities and it also constituted a test of the stallions' abilities and a means of selection. Thus only top class stallions with a marked aptitude for haute école are used as sires at the stud.

A training plan for the Spanish Riding School was drawn up at the end of the last century by Johann Meixner, the head riding master at that time, and by Field Marshal von Holbein, the deputy director of the institute. Previously handed down by word of mouth, the basic principles recorded here come under three main stages:

1. the forward gait
2. the lower (or campaign) school
3. the haute école

The forward gait entails working the horse at a walk, trot and canter on a long line. As yet, keeping the hooves together and shortening the gait is not required. The horse's stance is perfectly natural. The lower school is a development of the first stage. The horse is kept more in hand, thus achieving greater balance and the tractability required for all the various figures and turns. The haute école is the highest level of training for a dressage horse and is attained once the maximum degree of haunch bending and body lifting is achieved and once the horse can perform all the straightforward and complex gaits and raised exercises smoothly and regularly. He has been prepared for this during the first two stages.

Every autumn 8 to 10 young stallions from the stud at Piber are moved to the Spanish Riding School. Even for anyone familiar with daily life at the School there is something special about the first moment when these young horses enter the Renaissance courtyard of the stables for the first time. The director of the School and his staff wait to welcome the newcomers in the courtyard. Then the horses are given their first appraisal. The conduct of these young stallions provides some indication of their future potential. There follows a period of acclimatization, one to two weeks during which the four-year-old horses run free in the manège under the supervision of their future riders. Later they are lunged for several weeks and familiarized with the saddle. Soon the first rider is mounted on their back. This is all done with the greatest of care and consideration so that the horses learn to trust people and quickly become acquainted with the simplest indications.

The young horses are broken in with great care, for the Lipizzaner matures late and is not fully grown until the age of 7. The daily training period never exceeds 45 minutes, over-exertion being avoided. Moderation in the demands made on a horse during his youth allows him to maintain his capacity for work until he reaches a ripe old age. The 25-year-old stallions at the Spanish Riding School are by no means regarded as elderly horses. Years of systematic dressage work enable them to become fully developed physically so that they can easily cope with the demands made of them for many years. For the remainder of the year the young horses are ridden forward with increasing speed and are made more familiar with the rider's indications. During the second year of training more demands are gradually made of the stallion. Flexibility is promoted by practising turns and voltes. Sideways movements, passes and changes in gait and pace increase the degree of control. Cadence and timing of the steps improve. The stallion is already responsive to the most finely attuned guidance. At this stage the training of a School stallion does not differ basically from that of a dressage horse taking part in tournaments and entered for tests up to class M. In its third year of training the horse approaches the exercises of the haute école, a command of the lower school being a prerequisite here.

The haute école distinguishes between exercises on and above the ground. The movements on the ground include the piaffe, passage, pirouette and flying change. The movements above the ground consist of the pesade, levade, mezair, courbette, ballotade, croupade and capriole. All these exercises are movements drawn largely from nature, cultivated by training and turned to man's use. Horses out to graze display the loveliest passages or piaffes when they are excited. Fighting stallions often execute courbettes or jump with all four legs off the ground, striking at their opponent and thus demonstrating precise caprioles. Horses galloping freely change step in midflight at every change of direction in order to keep their balance.

The flying gallop change is prepared by leading the horse into a gallop from both sides. Then the gallop is practised with the change coming in the same place each time, so that the horse can learn the commands. Once it has grasped the regular gallop change, the stallion must frequently be ridden in a reverse gallop so that it can learn to change from the rider's guidance alone. In the pirouette the horse turns without changing his ground. The inner hind leg acts as a pivot for the forelegs and the outer hind leg. The piaffe is learnt in hand without a rider. From the shortened trot emerges the cadenced trot on the spot, the piaffe. There follows the piaffe with a rider, the latter merely sitting, quiet and relaxed, so that the horse gets used to a rider's weight while piaffing. Guidance is given by the instructor who stands beside the horse. Later he mounts so that he can actively encourage the horse.

The piaffe between the pillars precedes training in hand and with a rider. Work between the pillars, a method introduced by Pluvinel, often gives rise to misconceptions. It requires great skill, a sympathetic understanding of the horse and patience. The passage, or Spanish walk, is developed from the piaffe, the horse proceeding in the same rhythm and bringing the diagonally opposite legs to the ground at the same moment. The piaffe and the passage complete the haute école training on the ground. The horse is now eligible for class S dressage tests.

Not every stallion possesses the ability to perform levades and jumps. A talent of this kind is spotted during work between the pillars and the horses then receive specialized training in different exercises according to their individual aptitude. Years often elapse before the new generation yields a stallion with the talent to perform levades, courbettes or caprioles.

All the exercises are demonstrated in hand or with a rider and are performed without stirrups. The capriole is the most impressive movement performed above the ground. Work between the pillars is the best indication of a stallion's aptitude for this exercise. The most suitable horses are those which respond to every

Carousel in the "Presence of the Noble Allies", 1814

touch of the whip by striking out immediately with their hooves. The capriole has the following sequence: the rider leads his mount into a piaffe followed by a pesade and an exceptionally high ballotade. This ballotade becomes a capriole when the horse jerks out its hind legs together at the height of the leap. The whole movement is completed within a matter of seconds and demands the utmost concentration and effort on the part of horse and rider.

The Spanish Riding School — a byword for dressage horsemanship

It is impressive how the Spanish Riding School has always exerted an unmistakable influence on dressage tests at equestrian events.

The first name which must be mentioned here is that of Richard Wätjen who had the privilege of attending this fount of classical equestrianism as a guest pupil before the First World War. Here, Wätjen experienced the glorious era of Oberbereiter Meixner. His memoirs are full of sincere admiration for this head riding master who, according to Wätjen's reports, rode in inspired fashion with consummate stylishness, always presenting his horses with enormous dash and verve. Later Wätjen became a professional rider. His success as a rider and a trainer was great. A typical representative of the Viennese school, he worked his horses in strict accordance with its principles. His horses' piaffes and passages were exemplary.

Colonel Podhajsky, for many years the director of the Spanish Riding School, received his training at the School when a young officer in the dragoons. He learnt much from Oberbereiter Pollack and does not fail to make special mention of this head riding master in one of his books. On Nero, his thoroughbred, Colonel Podhajsky won the bronze medal at the 1936 Olympics in Berlin. For years now Christine Stückelberger of Switzerland has been working her horses under the supervision of former Oberbereiter Wahl whose abilities are a byword throughout the entire world of equestrianism. Granit and his charming rider have won everything that there is to win in international dressage. Granit's piaffes and passages are particularly striking and provide an obvious clue to his training.

Performances and guest performances

Originally performances were reserved for the Emperor's personal guests and were kept down to a fairly small scale. Later, at around the turn of the century, large sections of the population were admitted on special occasions. The Oberbereiter, or head riding master, rode several of the School stallions, demonstrating the exercises of the haute école on and above the ground. He also showed a horse exercising on the long rein. Sometimes a pas de deux was included and the performance always finished with a quadrille of four riders.

After the collapse of the Danube Monarchy the Spanish Riding School was compelled to make a considerable contribution to its own upkeep by giving more riding lessons and public performances. These performances were extended to include a display of work at the Riding School. The programme commences with a presentation of the young stallions, some of which still retain the dark coat of youth. They advance spiritedly, obediently accepting their riders' guidance. Then the fully trained stallions enter the manège, their riders paying homage to the portrait of Emperor Charles VI, the founder of the Winter Riding School. With incomparable grace they begin their work with all the paces and figures of the haute école. The horses are light on the reins and perform their piaffes, passages, pirouettes and gallop changes with amazing ease. They are followed by horses demonstrating their exercises in hand—piaffes along the edge of the arena and between the pillars, and school jumps without a rider. With the utmost obedience schooled stallions present pas de deux and pas de trois, performing all the figures and exercises with perfect accuracy. The work on the long rein is a speciality of the Spanish Riding School. The instructors walk on a level with the stallion's hind legs and demonstrate all the difficult exercises which have already been performed with a rider in the saddle. The horse responds to rein guidance alone. This work requires fully trained stallions obedient to the slightest touch. The figures above the ground are a special attraction for the spectators: leaping stallions execute their caprioles and courbettes or rise in a perfect levade. The traditional finale of a performance is always the great school quadrille with eight or twelve horses. It is a truly magnificent sight when these white horses perform their figures in unison, their supple movements harmonizing perfectly with their riders.

The circle of admirers of the Lipizzaners and the Spanish Riding School has constantly increased thanks to the guest performances given in Austria and abroad. Guest tours overseas would not be possible, had these superb horses not survived the turmoils of the past intact. Long journeys can now be managed by air and the haute école, that envoy of an ancient culture, conquers the hearts of spectators in the New World.

More than once the future of the Lipizzaner stud and the Spanish Riding School was at risk. That is why riders everywhere are grateful to Austria for ensuring that this future could become secure. With this gratitude goes the wish that the Lipizzaners and the Spanish Riding School may continue to be a byword for classical equestrianism and an example for horse lovers everywhere.

Brigadier Kurt Albrecht, seit Oktober 1974 Leiter der Spanischen Reitschule, und seine Mitarbeiter
Brigadier Kurt Albrecht, head of the Spanish Riding School since October 1974, together with his staff

Die Morgenarbeit in der Reithalle am Josefsplatz im Jahre 1890, Gemälde von Julius Blaas, 1890
Morning training in the Riding Hall in the Josefsplatz in 1890, painting by Julius Blaas, 1890

... etwa 90 Jahre später hat sich kaum etwas geändert
... some 90 years later hardly anything has changed

Nach alter Tradition wird auch immer ein brauner Hengst in der Spanischen Reitschule gearbeitet
According to old tradition one brown stallion is always kept at the Spanish Riding School

Am langen Zügel
On the long rein

Courbette an der Hand
Courbette in the hand

Pessade

Pas de trois
Pas de trois

Pas de deux, Piaffe

An der Stirnseite der Reithalle hängt ein zeitgenössisches Gemälde von Kaiser Karl VI. . . .
The wall facing the entrance to the Riding Hall bears a contemporary portrait of Emperor Charles VI . . .

. . . ihm, der die Reitschule erbauen ließ, gilt der Gruß beim Einreiten

he it is, the builder of the Riding School, to whom the riders pay homage on entering

Einreiten zur Quadrille, an der tête Oberst Handler, langjähriger Leiter der Spanischen Reitschule
Riding in for the quadrille, at the head Colonel Handler, for many years director of the Spanish Riding School

Die Schulquadrille

Großes Mohrenstechen in der Winterreitschule 1780, von Ignace Duvivier
Grand tournament in the Winter Riding School 1780, by Ignace Duvivier

Festliche Vorführung (Quadrille) etwa zweihundert Jahre später
Festive performance (quadrille) some two hundred years later